# QUANTUM COMPUTERS
## and Other Quantum Tech

Co-published by agreement between Shi Tu Hui and World Book, Inc.

Shi Tu Hui
Room 1807, Block 1,
#3 West Dawang Road
Chaoyang District, Beijing 100025
P.R. China

World Book, Inc.
180 North LaSalle Street
Suite 900
Chicago, Illinois 60601
USA

Copyright © 2024. All rights reserved. This volume may not be reproduced in whole or in part in any form without prior written permission from the publishers.

WORLD BOOK and the GLOBE DEVICE are registered trademarks or trademarks of World Book, Inc.

Library of Congress Cataloging-in-Publication Data for this volume has been applied for.

Cool Tech (set, hardcover)
ISBN: 978-0-7166-5479-7

Quantum Computers and Other Quantum Tech
ISBN: 978-0-7166-5484-1 (hardcover)
ISBN: 978-0-7166-5496-4 (softcover)
ISBN: 978-0-7166-5490-2 (e-book)

Written by Tom Jackson

## STAFF

VP, Editorial: Tom Evans
Manager, New Product: Nicholas Kilzer
Curriculum Designer: Caroline Davidson
Proofreader: Nathalie Strassheim
Coordinator, Design Development & Production: Brenda Tropinski
Digital Asset Specialist: Rosalia Bledsoe

Developed with World Book by
White-Thomson Publishing LTD
www.wtpub.co.uk

## ACKNOWLEDGMENTS

| | | | |
|---|---|---|---|
| Cover | © Dmitriy Rybin, Shutterstock | 24-25 | © Xanadu; © Erik Lucero, Google; © Zapp2Photo/Shutterstock |
| 5 | © Dmitriy Rybin, Shutterstock | 26-27 | © Xanadu |
| 6-7 | © solarseven/Shutterstock; © Larry Goldstein, D-Wave Systems | 28-29 | © Fouad A. Saad, Shutterstock; NIST; © Peter Schreiber Media/Shutterstock |
| 8-9 | © Jurik Peter, Shutterstock; © Erin Scott, IonQ; © agsandrew/Shutterstock | 30-31 | © D-VISIONS/Shutterstock; © Naeblys/Shutterstock; © sakkmesterke/Shutterstock |
| 10-11 | University of Science and Technology of China; © Calin H, Shutterstock; © Fouad A. Saad, Shutterstock; © asharkyu/Shutterstock | 32-33 | © ZinetroN/Shutterstock; © Vector Tradition/Shutterstock |
| 12-13 | © Quantinuum; © Chim/Shutterstock; © Forest Stearns, Google AI Quantum Artist in Residence; © Svitlana Kataieva, Shutterstock | 34-35 | © FastMotion/Shutterstock; © Naeblys/Shutterstock |
| | | 36-37 | © Andrea Danti, Shutterstock |
| | | 38-39 | © Mehdi Aslani |
| 14-15 | © IBM Research; © D-Wave Systems; © Kai Hudek, IonQ; © D-Wave Systems | 40-41 | © metamorworks/Shutterstock; © Golden Dayz/Shutterstock |
| 16-17 | © Peter Schreiber Media/Shutterstock; © James Teohart, Shutterstock | 42-43 | © Darkfoxelixir/Shutterstock; © Maksim Shmeljov, Shutterstock |
| 18-19 | © Xanadu; © StudioMolekuul/Shutterstock; © Vector Mine/Shutterstock | 44-45 | © ImageFlow/Shutterstock; © Jurik Peter, Shutterstock; © Esteban De Armas, Shutterstock; © Vac1/Shutterstock |
| 20-21 | © wk1003mike/Shutterstock; © Sergey Nivens, Shutterstock; © plotplot/Shutterstock | | |
| 22-23 | © BAIVECTOR/Shutterstock; © All is Magic/Shutterstock; © Ded Mityay, Shutterstock; © Evannovostro/Shutterstock | | |

# CONTENTS

Acknowledgments . . . . . . . . . . . . . . . . . . . . . . . . . . . . . .2

Glossary . . . . . . . . . . . . . . . . . . . . . . . . . . . . . . . . . . . . .4

Introduction . . . . . . . . . . . . . . . . . . . . . . . . . . . . . . . . . .5

1. Quantum Computing . . . . . . . . . . . . . . . . . . . . . . . . .6

2. Using Quantum Computers . . . . . . . . . . . . . . . . . . . 16

3. Quantum Simulators . . . . . . . . . . . . . . . . . . . . . . . . 26

4. Quantum Sensing . . . . . . . . . . . . . . . . . . . . . . . . . . 32

5. Quantum Communication . . . . . . . . . . . . . . . . . . . . 40

Resources . . . . . . . . . . . . . . . . . . . . . . . . . . . . . . . . . 46

Index . . . . . . . . . . . . . . . . . . . . . . . . . . . . . . . . . . . . . 48

There is a glossary of terms on the first page. Terms defined in the glossary are in boldface type **that looks like this** on their first appearance in the book.

# GLOSSARY

**artificial intelligence (AI)** the ability of a computer system to process information in a manner similar to human thought or to exhibit humanlike behavior.

**encryption** a procedure that changes a message to disguise it. A process called *decryption* is used to convert the disguised message back to its original form. Encryption has long been used in secret communication, such as in the sending of messages in code.

**entanglement** a special connection shared by particles in quantum mechanics. If two particles are entangled, an action performed on one of the particles instantly affects the state of the other, even if they are separated by vast distances.

**interferometry** a measurement method using superimposed waves (usually light, radio, or sound waves) to create an interference pattern, which can be measured and analyzed to obtain information.

**laser** a device that produces a narrow and intense beam of light of only one wavelength going in one direction. The special qualities of laser light make it ideal for a variety of applications.

**quantum mechanics** a branch of physics that describes the structure and behavior of matter. It has replaced classical mechanics, a group of older theories, as a description of the smallest known units of matter and their activity.

**quantum tunneling** a phenomenon of quantum mechanics in which a particle is able to penetrate through a potential barrier.

**silicon** a hard, dark-gray metalloid with a shiny luster. Silicon is a semiconductor, a material that conducts electric current better than an insulator like glass, but not as well as a conductor like copper. This property makes silicon especially useful in computer chips.

**subatomic particle** a unit of matter smaller than an atom. Subatomic particles include the three major particles found in atoms. Protons and neutrons form the nucleus of an atom. Electrons whirl about the nucleus.

**superconductivity** the ability of some materials to conduct electric current without resistance at extremely low temperatures. These materials, called superconductors, have many useful properties.

**superfluid** an exotic state of matter that acts like a liquid that flows absolutely freely. A superfluid has several unusual properties.

**superposition** the ability of a quantum system to be in multiple states at the same time until it is measured.

**teleportation** the transfer of matter or energy from one point to another without moving across the physical space between them.

**vacuum** a space that contains little matter.

# INTRODUCTION

Some inventions change history. A computer powered by microchip processors is one of the best examples. Few other innovations have had such an impact on the way we live. However, current computing technology is reaching a limit set by the laws of physics. Computer microprocessors have been made smaller and faster over decades. In turn, our devices have been getting more powerful and smarter. Today, a component on a microchip is about 7 nanometers (7 billionths of a meter), and billions of them will fit on a chip the size of a fingernail. Some experimental components are even smaller. However, soon it will not be possible to make these components any smaller. They are limited by the size of atoms themselves. We cannot make components smaller than atoms—so computers will stop getting smaller. Instead, to make computers smarter, we'll have to build them bigger. Or is there another way?

Down at the size of atoms—below around 1 nanometer—things start to behave very differently. Atoms and other tiny particles are ruled by a system called **quantum mechanics.** Scientists are now looking to build a new kind of computer— a quantum computer—that works using weird quantum rules. Quantum computers change what a computer can do in ways we are only just beginning to understand. Soon, the strange quantum realm may help develop new technologies used in scientific discovery, communication systems, and even teleporters!

# 1 QUANTUM COMPUTING

## COMPUTER REVOLUTION

The components of a quantum computer are very small. They are made from clusters of atoms or even a single atom. Yet a small quantum computer can be as powerful as a much larger classical computer (the type of computer we use today). But quantum computing technology has a long way to go before it becomes common. Current quantum computer designs are large and cumbersome devices that have limited capabilities.

Today, classical computing systems continue to do most tasks very well. And quantum computing may never completely replace the **silicon** chips of these classical systems for most devices. But scientists are not developing quantum computing simply to update the older classical systems. The exciting possibility is that once it is perfected, a quantum computer will be able to do things that are impossible for the largest and most powerful classical computers. For example, quantum computers may solve math problems that are too complicated for humans or classical computers. And what would an **artificial intelligence (AI)** driven by a quantum computer be capable of?

# THE QUANTUM WORLD

The main component of a classical computer is called a computer chip. This is a tiny piece of silicon that contains a complex electronic circuit. The circuit on a computer chip—sometimes called an integrated circuit—is made up of built-in electronic components. Most components serve as switches called transistors. A transistor is simply a switch that turns an electric current on and off. A transistor can turn on and off many thousands of times a second. However, it is always either on or off—never something in between. At the quantum scale, everything is much more uncertain. A quantum switch can easily be both on and off at once. This mind-boggling quality of quantum mechanics is what makes a quantum computer so incredibly powerful.

**Quantum objects.** The laws of quantum mechanics are used to understand how atoms and the smaller particles that make them up behave. All the matter around you is made of atoms. Atoms are made up of a central nucleus (core) of **subatomic particles** called protons and neutrons. Other particles called electrons orbit the nucleus of an atom. All these particles and atoms themselves are quantum objects. The laws of quantum mechanics dictate how they behave and interact.

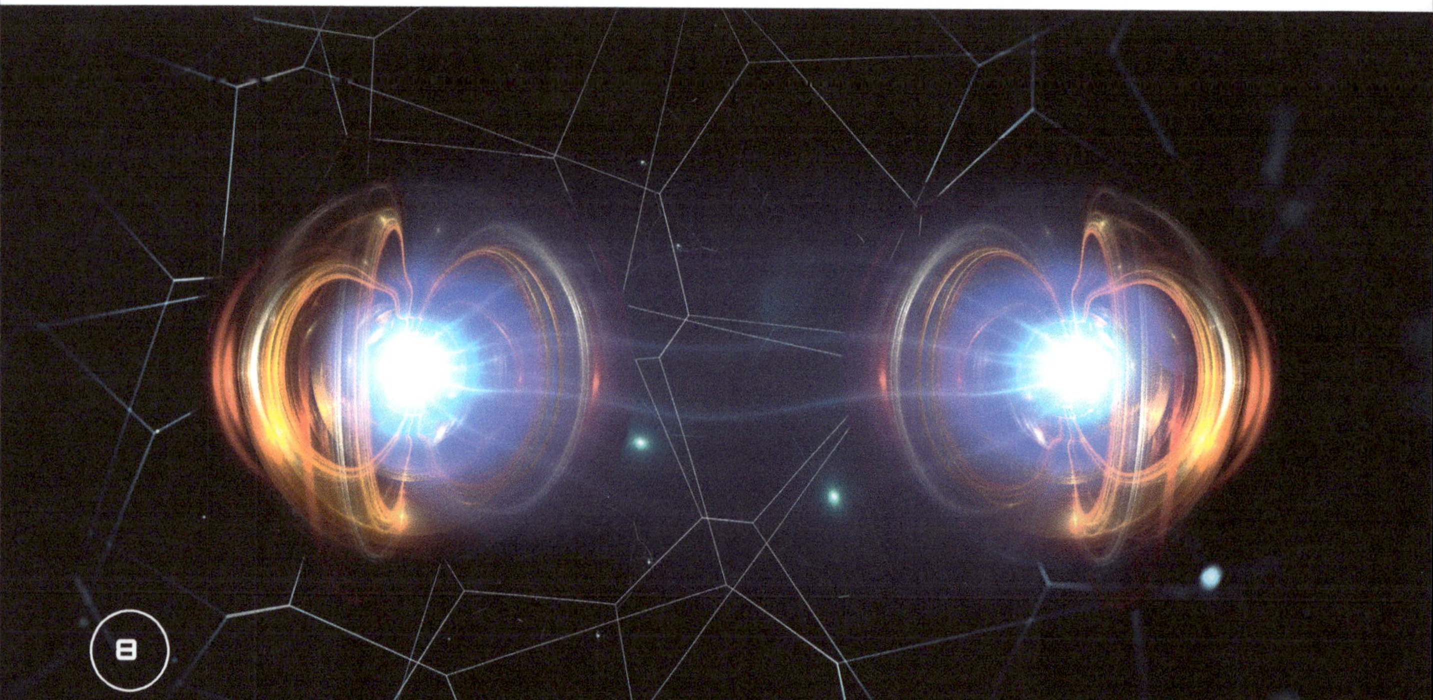

**Quantum effects.** What do scientists mean by the term *quantum*? The word simply refers to a very precise quantity that cannot be altered. The plural is quanta. Atoms and subatomic particles emit (give off) and absorb energy in discrete quantities, or quanta. The term *quantum mechanics* refers to the branch of physics that describes these smallest units of matter and their activity.

Quantum mechanics has allowed scientists to understand many aspects of the universe that are not easily explained by classical physics, for example, how light is produced and how chemicals interact with each other. But on a larger scale—the way we experience the world—quantum effects are not so clearly visible. There are so many atoms in a piece of matter that their activity merges into a single, predictable behavior. This behavior is adequately explained by classical physics. So, for example, when we turn on a switch, the light goes on. However, the behavior of an atom or a subatomic particle by itself is less clear and predictable —this is the quantum level. A quantum switch might be on or off. It may also be both on and off at the same time.

**A matter of chance.** In our everyday experience, we can measure any object in a number of ways. For example, a ball has size and weight, and we can measure how fast it is moving and in what direction. This is not possible in the quantum realm. Instead, quantum scientists use probability (the mathematics of chance) to describe a particle such as an electron. A particle might be moving in any direction. But you can only determine which directions are most likely. Under quantum rules, the particle's motion is a mixture of all possible speeds and directions—you cannot be sure.

**Uncertainty.** One of the most famous rules of quantum mechanics is the uncertainty principle. This rule states that the more we know about one behavior of a particle, the less we can know about another behavior. For example, if you precisely measure the speed of a particle, you cannot measure the direction of the particle with similar accuracy. It is possible to measure one aspect of a particle. But it is not possible to measure all aspects at once. This means that some aspects of a particle's behavior will always be uncertain.

# WHAT ARE QUBITS?

A computer is an information machine. All computers follow the same three simple steps. Step one is to receive an input of information. For step two, that information is processed according to the computer program (instructions). The processor is the device that does the actual computing in a computer. In step three, the processed information is output. The output may take any of a variety of forms, such as a video, a math solution, or a video game. The main difference between a classical computer and a quantum computer is the way they process information.

**Binary units.** In classical computing, information is encoded in units called bits. Bit is short for binary digit—a number written using only two digits, generally 1 and 0. The microchips used in the processors of today's classical computers typically handle information in chunks of 64 bits (a string of 64 1's and 0's). A typical home computer will have a few of these processors working together. The largest and fastest computers, call supercomputers, may use thousands of 64-bit processors at once. They can get pretty big. Thanks to the strange qualities of quantum mechanics, a quantum computer can encode more information with fewer processors.

**BIT**
*Classical Computing*

0

1

**QUBIT**
*Quantum Computing*

0

1

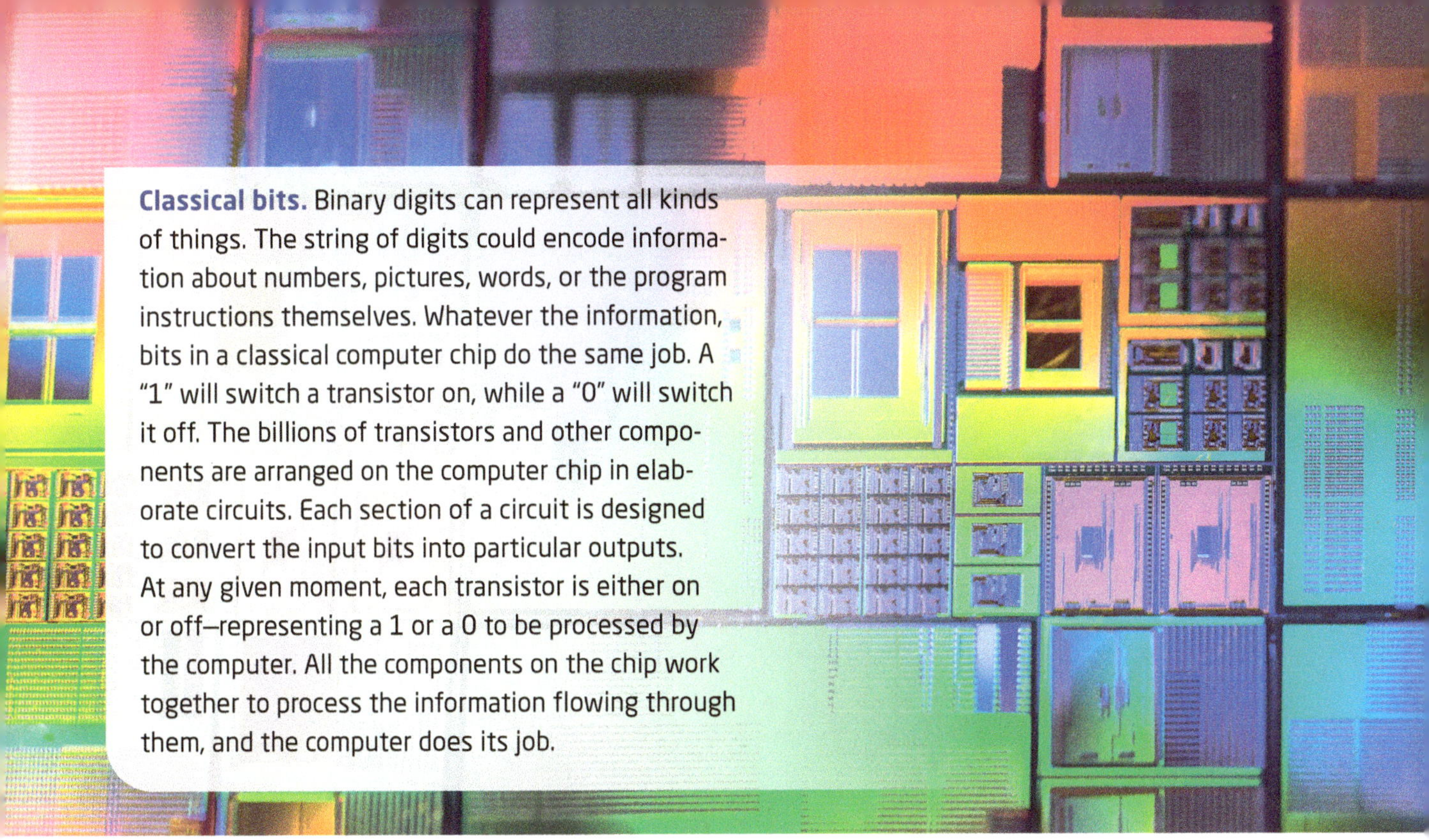

**Classical bits.** Binary digits can represent all kinds of things. The string of digits could encode information about numbers, pictures, words, or the program instructions themselves. Whatever the information, bits in a classical computer chip do the same job. A "1" will switch a transistor on, while a "0" will switch it off. The billions of transistors and other components are arranged on the computer chip in elaborate circuits. Each section of a circuit is designed to convert the input bits into particular outputs. At any given moment, each transistor is either on or off—representing a 1 or a 0 to be processed by the computer. All the components on the chip work together to process the information flowing through them, and the computer does its job.

**Quantum bits.** A quantum computer processor does not hold information in on-off switchlike units as a transistor does. Instead, it uses an atom or some other kind of quantum object to encode the information as a qubit. Qubit is short for quantum bit. Each qubit uses a quantum phenomenon called **superposition,** so that it represents both a 1 and a 0 at the same time. Subatomic particles, such as electrons, can exist in such ways. An electron has a quality called spin that can take the value "up" or "down." But the electron can also exist in a superposition of these states, in which its spin is both "up" and "down" at the same time. So a single electron can act as a qubit. However, the superposition collapses (becomes one state or the other) when the electron's spin is measured. For this reason, scientists can never directly observe superposition.

To make qubits into a computer processor, scientists make use of a quantum phenomenon called **entanglement.** This occurs when two quantum objects are linked. When one object changes its state in some way, the other will always change as well. Quantum computing takes advantage of superposition and entanglement to compute in fundamentally new ways. However, quantum entanglement is unstable. Maintaining superposition or entanglement for even a few seconds of computing time remains a difficult engineering problem.

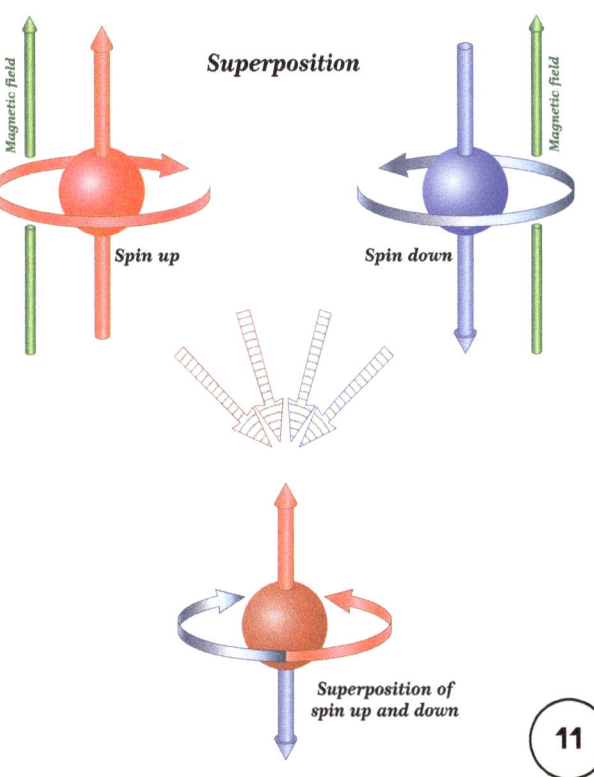

# PROCESSING POWERS

Data is another word for the information handled by computers. A classic 64-bit computer chip, like the ones used in modern smartphones or laptops, can send and receive chunks of data trillions of times every second. But the chip can only hold 64 bits of data at any one time. This limits what the computer processor can process, so complex tasks are processed slowly. This works fine for most everyday computer function, like streaming video and searching the internet. But such future technologies as artificial intelligence, robotics, and self-driving cars require a faster computing system. That's where a quantum processor can revolutionize technology—such a device could process huge amounts of data with astounding speed.

**Binary code.** Binary code uses only bits—the digits 0 and 1—to represent all numbers. So, even small numbers must be represented by a string of bits. Larger numbers require even longer strings. For example, in binary digits, the number 2 is represented as 10—a 1 and a 0. The number 4 is represented as a 1 and two 0's (100). In binary digits, the number 64 is represented as 1000000. It's easy to see how the binary code for larger numbers can get very big indeed. One of the great advantages of a quantum computer is that it can hold much more data in this form compared to a classical computer.

**Units of data.** A bit is the smallest unit of data used by a computer—it is either a 1 or a 0. Early electronic computers could hold 8 bits of data at a time. A set of 8 bits (8b) is called 1 byte (1B), and 16 bits is 2 bytes, and so on. Bytes—and not the smaller bits they are made of—are the building blocks for computer information. Larger numbers of bytes are counted up as kilobytes (1,000 bytes), megabytes (1 million bytes), and gigabytes (1 billion bytes). In classical computing, the number of bits corresponds exactly to the number of electronic components on a microchip. A 1-gigabyte memory stick has 8 billion units for storing 8 billion bits of data. It's quite straightforward.

**Processing power.** The processing power of a quantum computer is related to the number of qubits in a different way. One bit can represent either a 1 or a 0, while a qubit can represent both a 1 and a 0 at the same time—so it holds twice as much information. When 2 classical bits are put together, they can hold 2 bits of data, one of these four possible sets: 0,0; 0,1; 1,0; 1,1. But 2 qubits can hold all four of these sets at once. The amount of data 2 qubits hold is 22 = 4 bits. The pattern continues with 3 qubits holding 23 bits—equal to 8 bits or 1 byte of data.

Going further, the processing power goes up very fast indeed. An 8-bit classical computer holds 8 bits of data. That is enough to store any number from 0 to 255. But an 8-qubit system holds 28 or 256 bits of data. It can hold any number from 0 to 11,579,208,923,731,619,542,357,098,500,868,790! A 13-qubit processor can hold more than 8,000 classical bits. Meanwhile, a 64-qubit system could handle 18,446,744 trillion bits of data all at once

# QUANTUM COMPUTING HARDWARE

The theory behind quantum computers is astounding, but putting the theory into practice is not at all easy. In 2022, the American-based International Business Machines Corporation (IBM) unveiled Osprey, a 433-qubit quantum computer processor. IBM is developing even larger and more powerful quantum processors. But keeping the qubits entangled and working together is a major technological challenge. Quantum processors need to be shielded from the outside world to work. Thus, new designs for computer hardware are needed.

**Isolation.** For a quantum chip (processor) to do its job, computer scientists need to know the state of each qubit and keep the qubits entangled, so that they can store data. Qubits are unstable and can be disturbed by heat, vibrations, magnetism, light, and other electromagnetic waves from smartphones, radio equipment, or satellites. Therefore, a quantum chip is shielded inside layers of protective materials and metals. The quantum chip is held in a perfect **vacuum** at the center. Control systems are connected to the chip through superconducting wires.

**Supercool.** Unlike regular electrical equipment, superconducting wires give off no heat as the electrical current runs through them. They work best when they are very cold—so quantum computers often resemble refrigerators. Quantum computer components may be cooled to nearly the lowest temperature possible, known as absolute zero: -459 °F (-273 °C). That's colder than outer space! The deep cold also helps control the qubits and keep them entangled.

**Ion trap.** Since qubits are made up of atoms or subatomic particles, there are several ways to construct one. One qubit design uses a single metal atom with an electron removed. That turns the atom into a charged particle called an ion. A **laser** beam is used to control another electron orbiting the ion. The beam delivers the exact quantum (amount) of energy needed to move the electron away from the ion and return. Using light to control particles like this is called photonics. The photonic system is used to input data to the qubit, which is entangled with other qubits to create a processor.

**Superconductor loops.** Another qubit design uses two loops of superconducting wires. The wires are brought very close together to create a quantum effect where a current runs between the wires. The current in an ordinary device needs to be pushed through a wire by an electrical force known as voltage. But the current can move through the superconducting loop without voltage. The flow of current back and forth between the loops is used to represent bits of data.

**Silicon quantum dot.** A final qubit design is a single electron held within a tiny crystal of silicon. Electrical effects are used to control the electron so it acts as a transistor. This design is most similar to today's microchips, which are also made up of tiny components made from pieces of silicon. Such quantum dot qubits could be made millions of times smaller than current computer chips, and quantum computers could contain thousands of them.

# 2 USING QUANTUM COMPUTERS

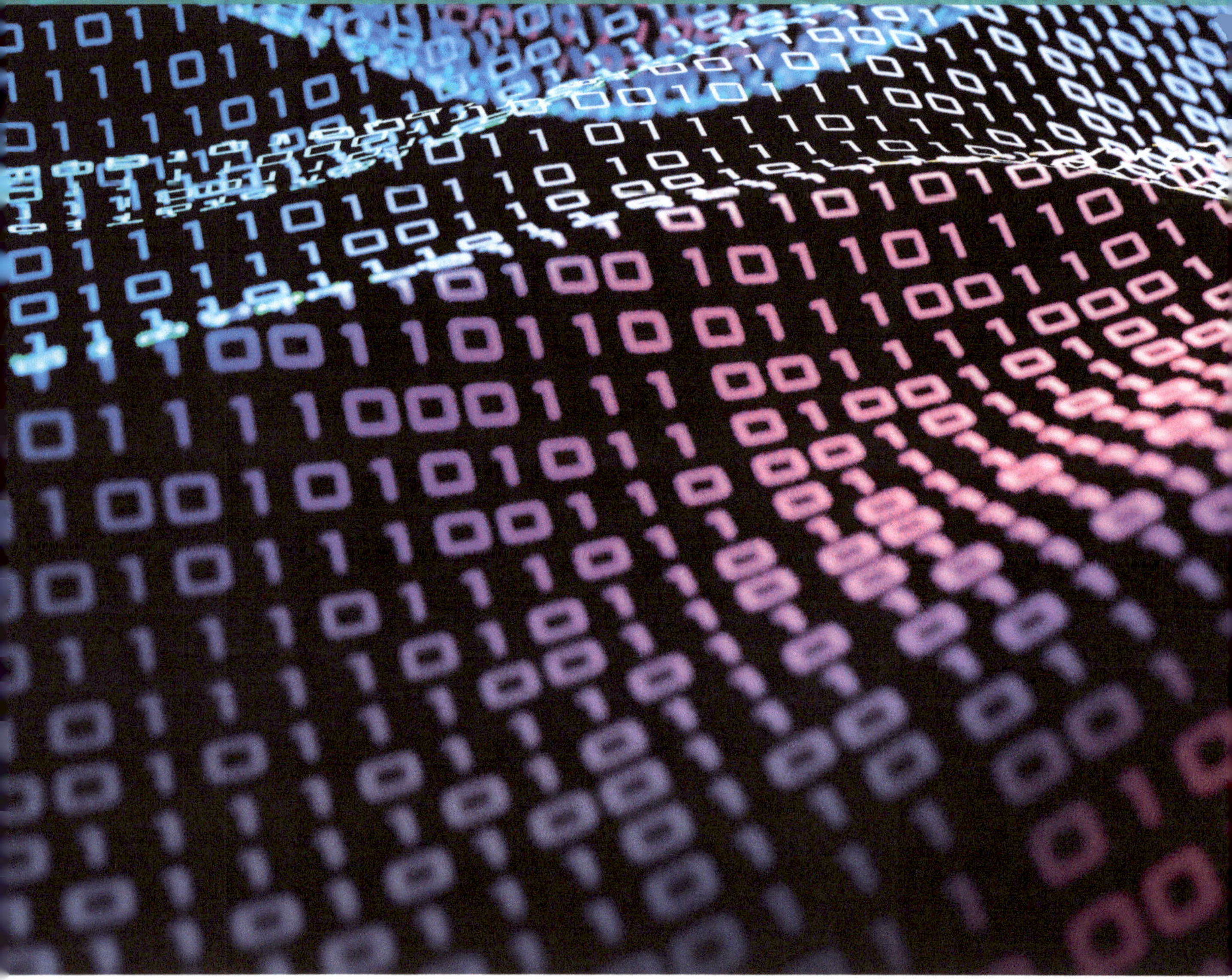

## QUANTUM ALGORITHMS

An algorithm is a set of mathematical instructions set out in a logical order. If followed correctly, it will transform an input into the correct output time after time. Although algorithms are a very old idea dreamed up by ancient mathematicians, the word is closely associated with the way modern computer technology works. Computer programs are essentially algorithms. An algorithm is deciding what appears on your social media feed right now. Others convert binary code to the sound in your headphones, control the dishwasher, and manage your city's traffic signals. A quantum computer could run these algorithms perfectly well. But the weird effects of quantum mechanics mean that quantum computers can do much more. So-called quantum algorithms can make use of qubit superposition to perform tasks much faster than classical computers—and perhaps do things that are not possible with current computers. Computer scientists already have a clear idea of what some quantum algorithms can do. But there is much yet to discover. Most experts agree that quantum computing can dramatically change technology and even civilization.

## HARD PROBLEMS

It is an interesting quirk of history that classical computers arose from a math puzzle about algorithms. About 90 years ago, the British scientist Alan Turing imagined a machine that could take in information and give out answers. Turing's idea became the basic design for today's computers. Turing showed that some algorithms never find an answer. A computer running such an algorithm would continue processing forever. Other algorithms will take a very long time to calculate output—perhaps millions of years. And there was no way of telling how long it would take to get an answer without trying them out. Computer scientists describe algorithms like this as "hard problems." But quantum algorithms may make some of these hard problems a lot easier and solve them much faster.

**Hard math.** Mathematicians divide math problems into two groups called P and NP. The puzzles in the P group can be solved given enough time. A P problem might take a computer a long time, but it will eventually calculate the answer. Using a more powerful computer will speed up the process. An NP math problem does have an answer, but it would take a classical computer an almost infinite amount of time to find it. As the NP problem is being solved, more and more possible answers are created, and each one needs to be checked. However, if we did have an answer to the problem, it would be simple to check that it is correct. An example of an NP problem is whether all sudoku grids of any size can be solved. It's impossible to know without checking them all, and the grids go on forever. Some NP problems will be just as difficult for quantum computers as classical ones, but there is a subgroup of problems—called NP-hard problems—that might be unlocked by quantum algorithms.

# QUANTUM TUNNELING

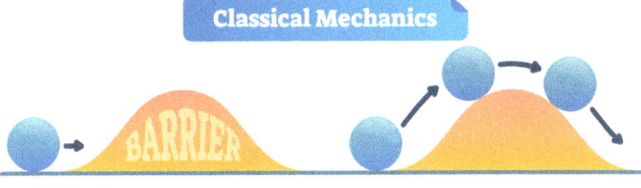

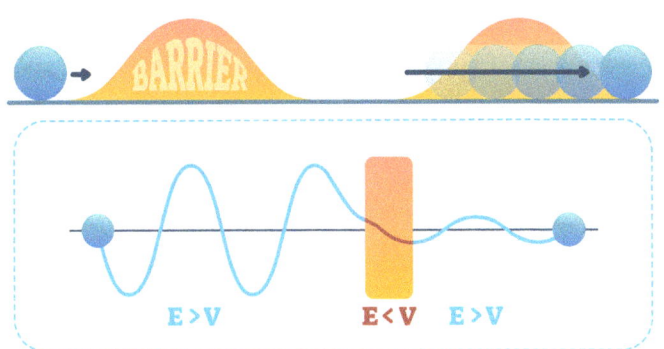

**Quantum annealing.** NP-hard problems are often about finding links between sets of data. A famous NP-hard puzzle is called the Traveling Salesman Problem. This involves calculating the best route for a traveling salesperson, so they travel the least distance in the shortest time. The same method could be used to link computer data for use by social media, internet search engines, or artificial intelligence. However, to solve this puzzle, we'd need to check every possible route and connection to find the best ones. Quantum algorithms can use a process called annealing to predict which routes are most likely to be best. Annealing makes use of **quantum tunneling,** which is a phenomenon where particles take shortcuts through space. A quantum algorithm could use tunneling to find the links in data and find shortcuts to the answer to a hard problem.

**Protein folding.** Proteins are molecules that make up the body of living things. There are many different kinds of protein. Each has a specific and complex shape determined by its chemical structure. A single change to the chemical structure results in a change in the overall shape of the protein, altering the function. Scientists consider calculating a protein's shape from its chemical structure an NP-hard problem. However, a powerful AI program developed by Google named AlphaFold solved the problem in 2020. Thanks to AlphaFold, biochemists can now design proteins and other complex chemicals to make new medicines. AlphaFold uses a classical computer algorithm. A quantum computer could solve this NP-hard problem even faster.

## ATTACKING ENCRYPTION

Quantum computing may create difficulties by breaking **encryption**—the security systems used in telecommunications. Encryption is a procedure that changes a message to disguise it. Encryption has long been used in secret and secure communication. Encryption is used to protect transactions made over an ATM (automated teller machine) network or the internet. It prevents wrongdoers from intercepting bank account numbers, credit card numbers, or other personal data during transactions. Encryption relies on complex mathematical calculations that are difficult to solve or reverse. However, quantum computers promise to solve such calculations easily and break any encryption. What will happen then?

**Codes and keys.** Today, computer encryption programs translate data into a code that replaces words, phrases, or sentences with groups of letters or numbers. A process called decryption is used to convert the disguised message back to its original form. A code is only as secure as its key—the method used to encrypt and decrypt the information. Two people can communicate in private if they each have a key. But to start their conversation, one must give the other the key. If the key is sent through the internet, someone else might see it. That third person can then use the key to read the private messages.

Internet encryption typically uses two number keys. One number is public, and the other is private. The public key is shared in messages and used to convert it into codes. However, it is only possible to decrypt the coded message using the private key.

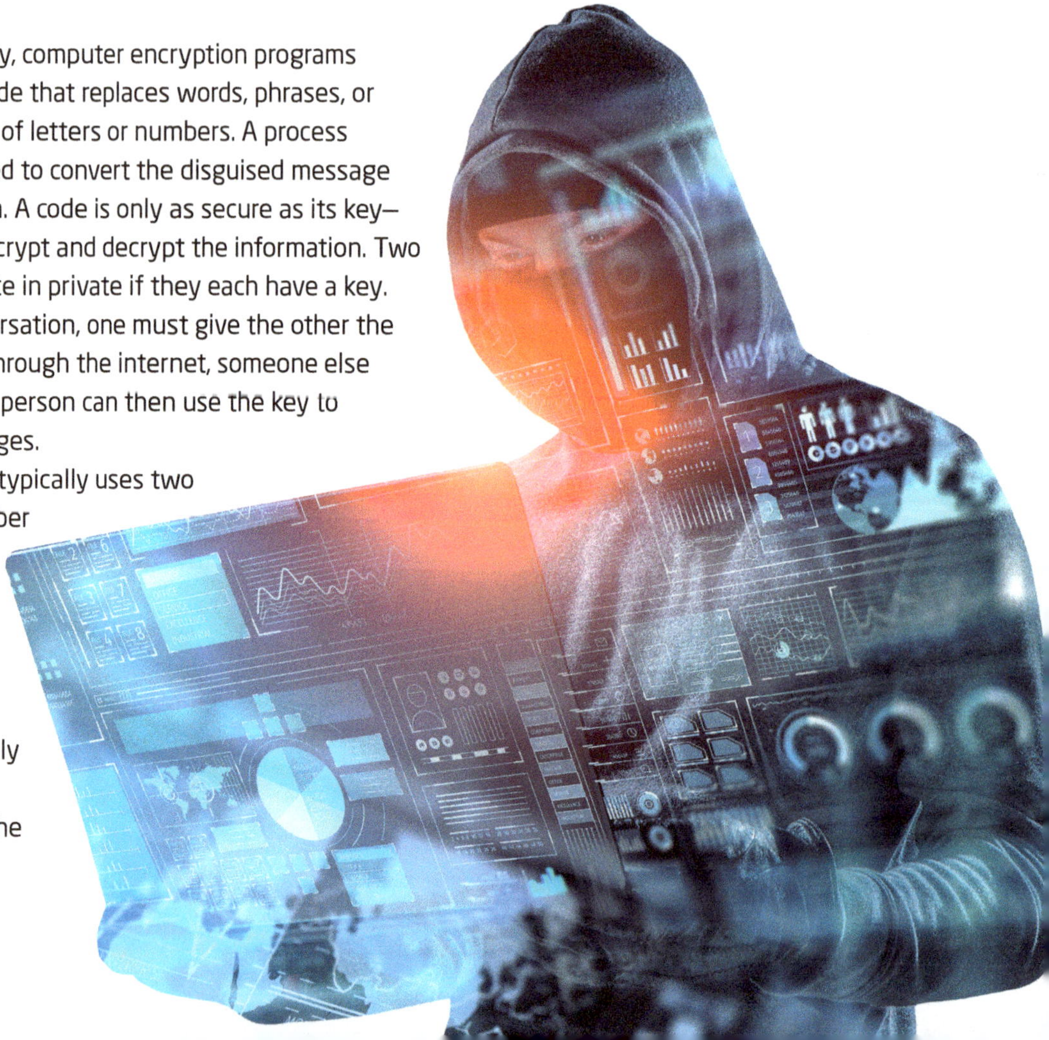

**Brute force attack.** The numbers used for both public and private keys are often made by multiplying two large prime numbers (numbers only divisible by themselves and 1). The prime numbers used have hundreds of digits. To break the encryption, you could take the public key and calculate the two original prime numbers. You can then calculate the private key and read the secret message. However, those calculations are done through trial and error—as every combination of prime numbers is checked one by one. This method of cracking encryption is called a brute force attack. It would take a classical computer about 300 trillion years to crack an everyday encryption system. That's why it is so secure. But the immense processing power of a quantum computer could crack the encryption much faster. Will future quantum computers solve encryption fast enough to threaten all encryption?

**The end of encryption?** Quantum computers are unlikely to end encryption anytime soon. Even if a quantum computer was one million times faster at cracking encryption than is possible today, it would still take 300 million years to break a typical code! Computer scientists estimate that a quantum computer with 20 million qubits would take just 8 hours to crack the code. But the largest quantum computers today have just around one thousand qubits. Quantum processors powerful enough to break encryption and threaten online security are probably decades away. By then, scientists expect quantum computers to use advanced encryption systems that are also based on quantum technology.

# QUANTUM INTELLIGENCE

Quantum computers promise to take artificial intelligence (AI) to amazing new levels. Artificial intelligence (AI) is the ability of a computer system to process information like human thought or to exhibit humanlike behavior. An AI computer system can teach itself how to do a task. As the system "learns," the AI program writes and rewrites its own algorithm. This process is called machine learning. Quantum machine learning will not only be faster, but the properties of such systems promise breakthroughs in our understanding of human intelligence.

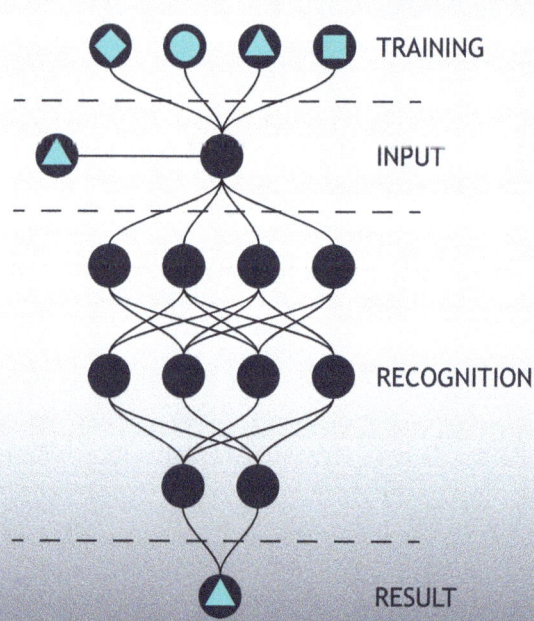

**Basic machine learning.** An AI uses a processor called a neural network to learn how to do a task. The neural network is a series of nodes connected in many layers. An input can travel through the network along many different paths from node to node. AI will direct the input along a particular path based on the data it contains. For example, if the AI is asked to identify pictures of faces, the data that contains facelike shapes will be sent along the path, which then creates the correct output.

But the AI must first learn what to look for. To "train" the AI, the program is fed picture data—some with faces and some without. Through trial and error, the AI "learns" to identify facelike shapes. Eventually, the neural network will be able to identify a face. The AI never gets tired or bored. With each picture, it learns how to do its job better. Eventually, the AI will identify faces better than any human can.

**Quantum machine learning.** Machine learning requires a lot of computer processing power. AI programs run through classical computers take months to train themselves for specific tasks. A quantum AI processor could sort larger quantities of data and learn much faster and more efficiently. Could quantum phenomena also help quantum AI become more intelligent than a classical AI? Machine learning uses the mathematics of chance (probability) to decide how to classify picture data as "face" or "no face." In a quantum computer, qubits could classify the data as both at the same time through superposition. The quantum AI will only opt for a final answer when all the other qubits agree—and that occurs with amazing speed. Processors using quantum tunneling and entanglement may also find links in the data that classical AI cannot detect.

**Theory of intelligence.** Computer scientists divide AI programs into two types—narrow AI and general AI. Narrow AI learns to do a specific set of tasks, such as searching for faces or listening to voice commands. Narrow AI can accomplish these tasks very well. But narrow AI does not know that there are tasks it cannot do. A general AI "knows" that there are things that it does not know. General AI can determine what it must learn to fill this knowledge gap. Currently, all AI programs are narrow. Some computer scientists doubt that general AI is even possible in a computer system. General AI is similar to human intelligence and consciousness—we are aware that human minds are different and that people think about different things in different ways. Where does human consciousness come from? Some scholars think consciousness emerges from the complex activity of the human brain. If this is correct, could a quantum AI that processed as much data as a human brain become conscious? Computer and AI scientists call this the technological singularity. What would happen next? How would such a quantum singularity relate to humans? Could a quantum AI singularity become a threat to humans?

# QUANTUM SUPREMACY

Quantum computers are still in their early stages, as engineers race to figure out how to make larger qubit processors. As technology improves, quantum computers will eventually replace classical computers and also perform tasks that are currently impossible with today's computers. This event is called quantum supremacy. When will quantum supremacy happen—or has it already happened?

**The battle for supremacy.** There are many competitors in the race for quantum computing supremacy. These include software companies like Google and Microsoft, computer manufacturers like IBM and Intel, and universities and institutes, such as the Chinese Academy of Science and the Massachusetts Institute of Technology (MIT). Many have announced recent breakthroughs in quantum computing. These include creating newer, faster quantum processors using hundreds and even thousands of qubits. The pace of development is impressive. For example, in 2019, Google's Sycamore processor used 53 qubits. Using superconducting qubits, in 3 minutes the device can perform calculations for which a classical computer would require 2.5 days. In 2021, Chinese scientists unveiled their 66-qubit Zuchongzhi 2 quantum computer. This machine also uses superconducting qubits and is up to one million times faster than Sycamore. In 2022, IBM unveiled Osprey, their latest quantum device, which uses 433 superconducting qubits. IBM also plans to produce Condor, a quantum computer that uses 1,000 qubits, by 2025. All these devices claim to surpass classical computers—and each other. But has quantum supremacy been achieved?

**Quantum practicality.** Quantum supremacy is not the biggest prize. To achieve quantum supremacy, a device needs only to surpass the calculating abilities of a classical computer once. It might not be able to repeat such a feat without extensive preparation. The quantum processors are all still largely experimental and not yet reliable enough for practical use. Computer engineers struggle to keep the qubits in these processors entangled and working together for more than a fraction of a second.

The milestone when quantum devices become reliable is called quantum practicality. Intel Corporation is taking a different approach to quantum practicality by building processors using silicon quantum dot qubits. These are much smaller than other qubit designs, and they can be placed on computer chips in large numbers. Not all the Intel qubits will be entangled at once. But enough will be entangled so that the device will reliably process data. Accurately ensuring that qubits are entangled and detecting those that are not working properly remains an important obstacle to achieving quantum practicality.

**Quantum memory.** A quantum computer needs a quantum memory system to store whatever the processor outputs. In a classical computer, this component is called the RAM, or random access memory. The information released by a quantum processor is represented by the quantum state of a particle, such as a photon (the subatomic particle that makes up light). The quantum memory must hold this particle in an unchanging state and send it to the processor when needed. Quantum computer engineers achieve this by storing information in the photons of laser beams that bounce inside clouds of gas.

# 3 QUANTUM SIMULATORS

## STUDYING NATURE

Quantum mechanics is one of the most successful scientific theories. However, scientists still do not fully understand all things in the quantum realm. Investigating the science of quantum phenomena is technologically challenging. Quantum simulators create certain conditions in atoms and ions, so that quantum behaviors of these objects can be observed by scientists to test theories in quantum mechanics. Quantum simulators share some features of quantum computers. The technology provides a close-up view of the strange quantum world.

# INVESTIGATING QUANTUM PHENOMENA

Scientists use the same tech used to make qubits for quantum computers to simulate and study strange quantum phenomena. Like a quantum computer, a quantum simulator relies on the entanglement of quantum objects—atoms, ions, or subatomic particles. Scientists can study the behavior of these quantum objects in different experiments. A quantum simulator captures the quantum phenomena and expresses it in such a way that scientists can observe and record the strange properties that emerge.

**Deep cooling.** Quantum simulators demonstrate the fascinating quantum phenomena that appear in matter at extremely low temperatures—such as superfluidity and **superconductivity.** Ordinary refrigeration systems are not powerful enough to cool substances enough to study the quantum realm. Instead, scientists use laser cooling and magnetic traps to create the coldest temperatures ever recorded.

Laser cooling uses the qualities of quantum mechanics to steal energy from particles and make them colder. A laser is a focused beam of light made up of packets of energy called photons. Photons are taken in and given off by other particles—such as atoms—under certain conditions. When a laser photon strikes an atom in a certain way, it can carry away some energy from that particle. When atoms lose energy, they cool.

Scientists trap particles inside a magnetic field to make things even colder. The particles with the most energy—and the highest temperatures—will bounce out of this magnetic trap, leaving only the most sluggish and coldest particles behind. At the very coldest temperatures, individual atoms merge into a liquidlike form called a condensate. Scientists study condensates to understand how certain phenomena, including gravity, work on the quantum scale.

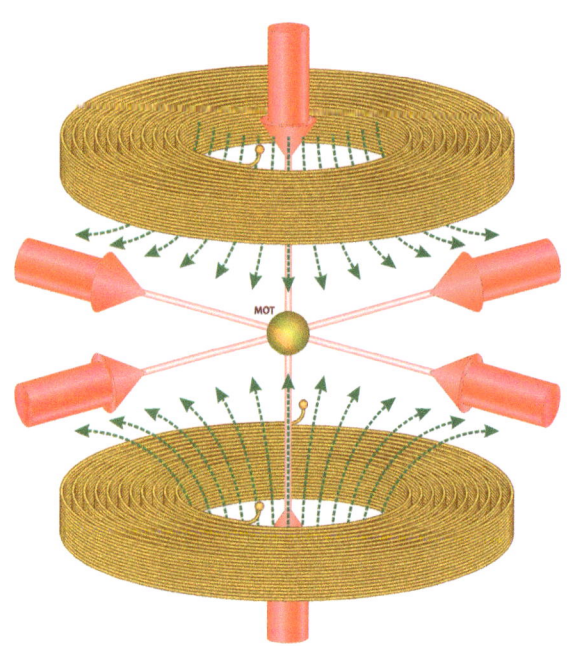

**Super substances.** Several unusual quantum behaviors appear in certain substances that are cooled to almost absolute zero. Some materials become superconductors—that is, they conduct electric current without any resistance. Superconductors have important applications in quantum computers and other advanced technologies. Scientists still do not fully understand how superconductivity occurs.

**Superfluid.** Superfluidity is another quantum phenomenon that only appears when a liquid is super cold. In normal conditions, all liquids resist flow—a property called viscosity. Fluids with high viscosity, such as honey, flow more slowly than those with low viscosity, such as water. But at very cold temperatures, some substances become **superfluid** and have no viscosity at all. Nothing will stop the flow of a superfluid—it will flow uphill and up the walls of a container!

**Time crystals.** The atoms that make up certain crystals show other quantum properties when very cold. At extremely low temperatures, the atoms in certain crystals vibrate without energy. The crystal cannot get any colder, but its atoms cannot stop moving. This creates a clocklike system called a time crystal where the atoms move back and forth—like a watch crystal in perfect time forever. Scientists think that these properties could make them useful as a future form of quantum memory.

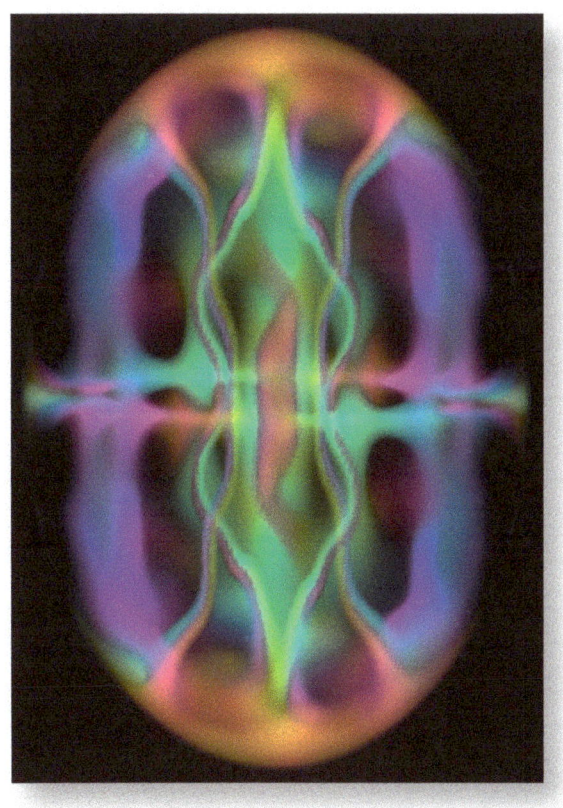

**Wave simulations.** Physicists today can turn a quantum particle into a math equation called a wave function. The wave function mathematically describes all the features of the particle and shows what it is likely to do next. But the math gets very complicated when many particles are described at once. A change in one particle will alter all the other wave functions around it. Quantum computers could handle this complicated math to simulate many wave functions—promising a new way to study quantum mechanics.

# PARTICLE COLLIDERS

Scientists study quantum mechanics and the particles that make up the universe using a complex machine called a particle accelerator (also called a particle collider). A particle accelerator is a huge device designed to accelerate particles of matter to an extremely high velocity and then collide them. Scientists study the energy released and the particles produced by the collisions to learn about the nature and properties of atoms and subatomic particles. The high-speed collisions briefly recreate the conditions that exist inside stars and the conditions that existed in the earliest moments of the universe. This kind of quantum research requires the largest and most powerful machines on Earth.

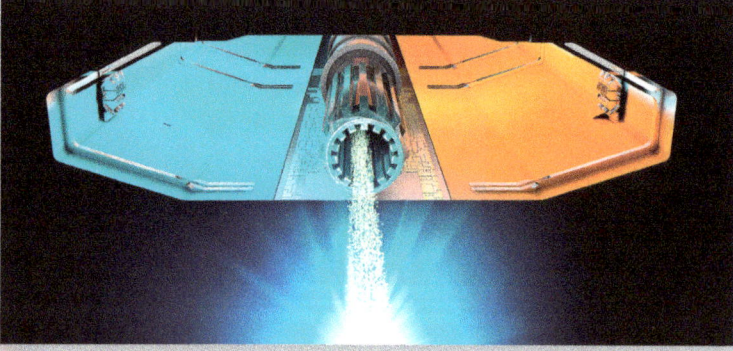

**Acceleration.** Before particles can be smashed together effectively in a collider, they must be accelerated to very high speeds. The world's largest particle collider is the Large Hadron Collider (LHC)—a ring measuring more than 16.5 miles (27 kilometers) outside Geneva, Switzerland. The collider generates two beams of particles and uses more than 9,000 superconducting magnets to steer the beams through the ring in opposite directions. Powerful electric fields accelerate the particles to near the speed of light. LHC guides the two particle beams into collisions at several places around the ring. At these locations, giant detectors record other particles produced by the collisions. China's planned Circular Electron Positron Collider (CEPC) will be an even larger—62 miles (100 kilometers)—and more powerful collider.

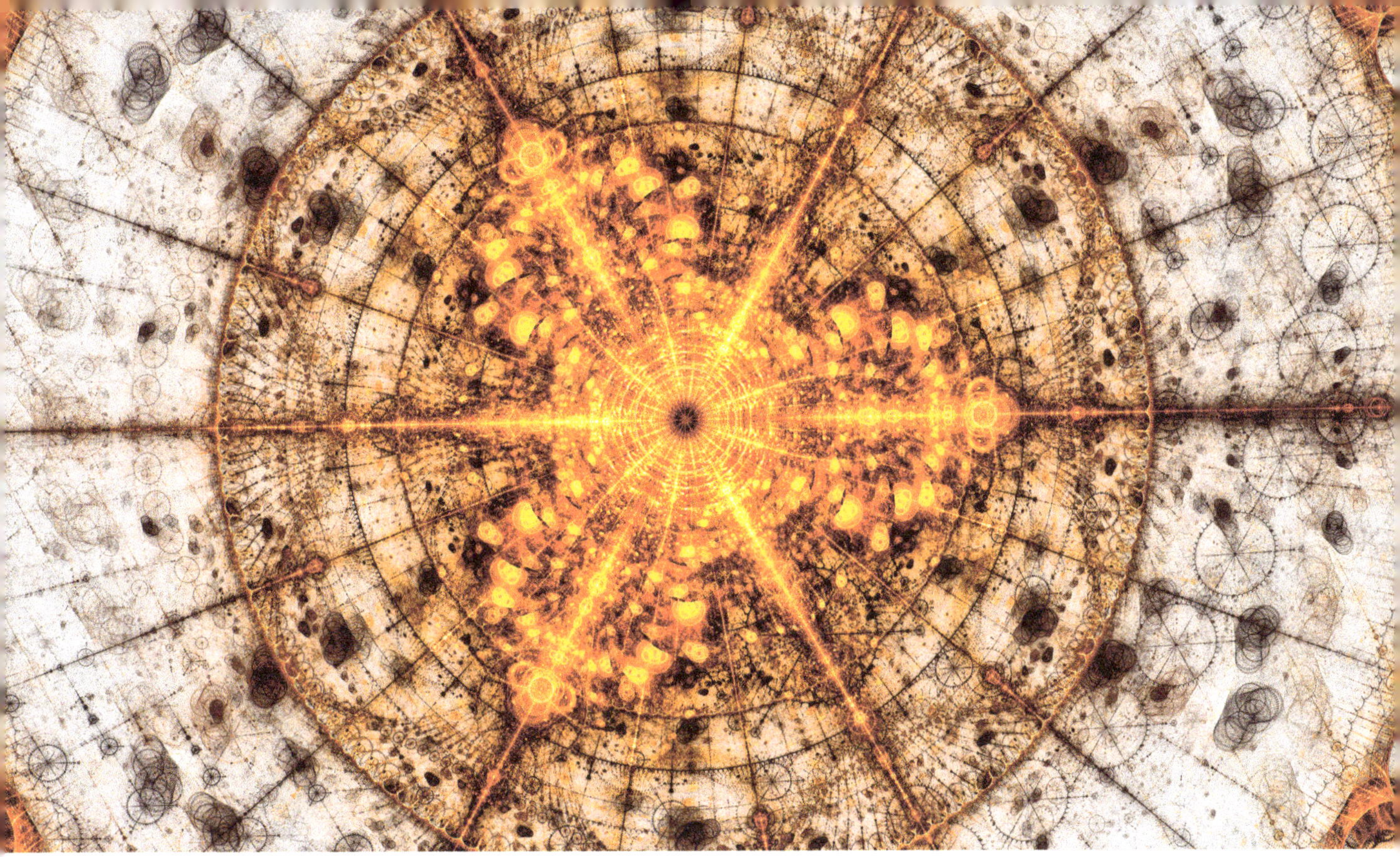

**Detectors.** Scientists have developed a wide variety of detectors for observing the particles that emerge from the incredibly energetic collisions that occur in these machines. When the particles collide, energy is released, and quantum particles spray out in all directions. The particles pass through layers of materials that produce an electric signal when a particle passes through them. As they pass, different particles create tiny electric currents in particular layers. This allows scientists to track the path of each particle. Scientists can identify a particle from this electrical signature, the route it takes, and the particle's speed.

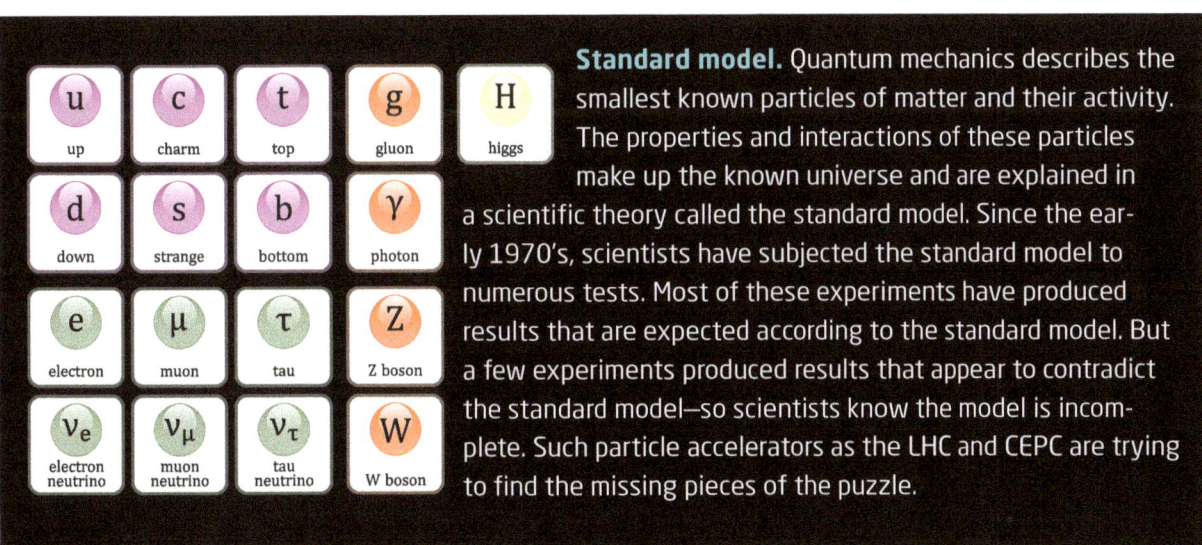

**Standard model.** Quantum mechanics describes the smallest known particles of matter and their activity. The properties and interactions of these particles make up the known universe and are explained in a scientific theory called the standard model. Since the early 1970's, scientists have subjected the standard model to numerous tests. Most of these experiments have produced results that are expected according to the standard model. But a few experiments produced results that appear to contradict the standard model—so scientists know the model is incomplete. Such particle accelerators as the LHC and CEPC are trying to find the missing pieces of the puzzle.

# 4 QUANTUM SENSING

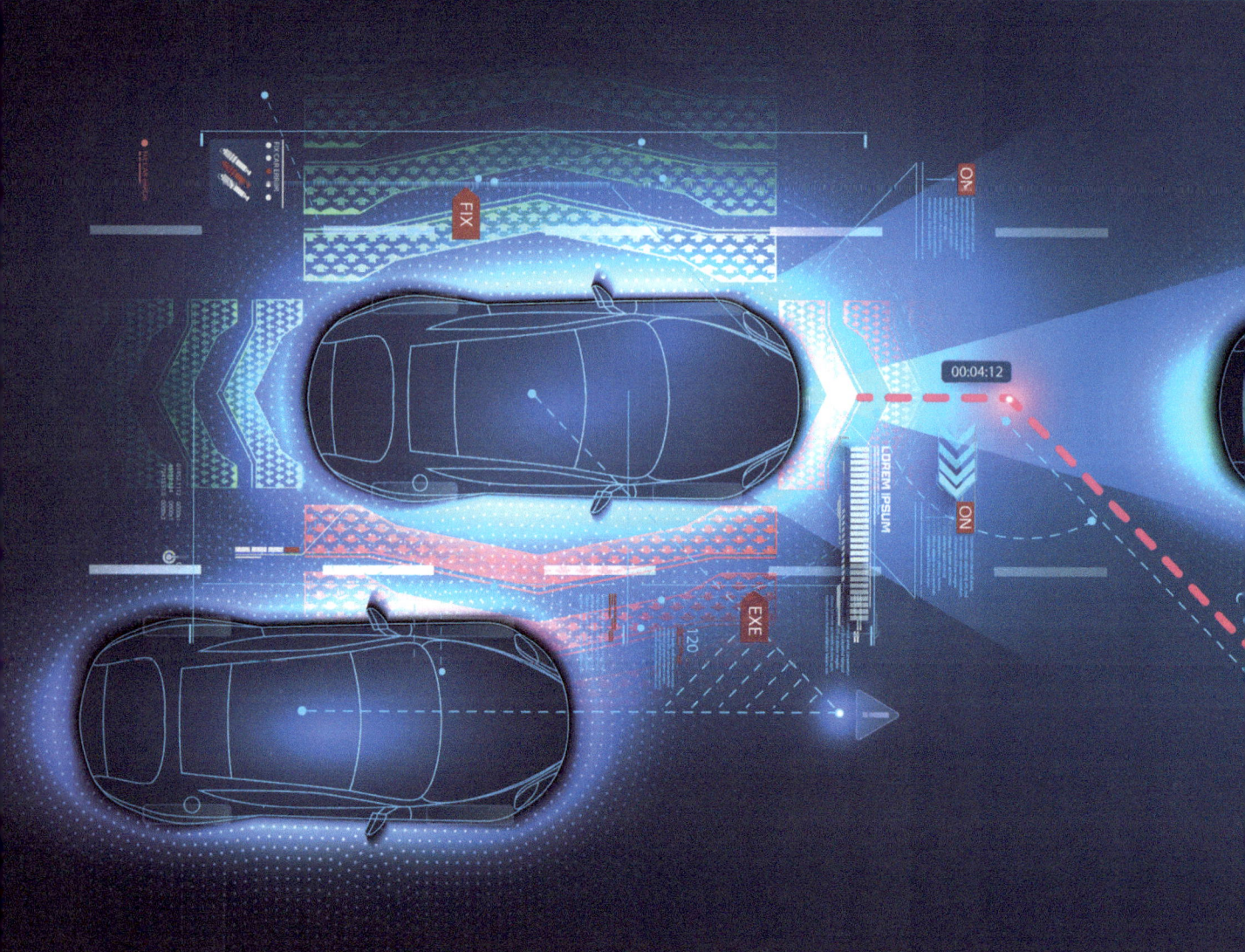

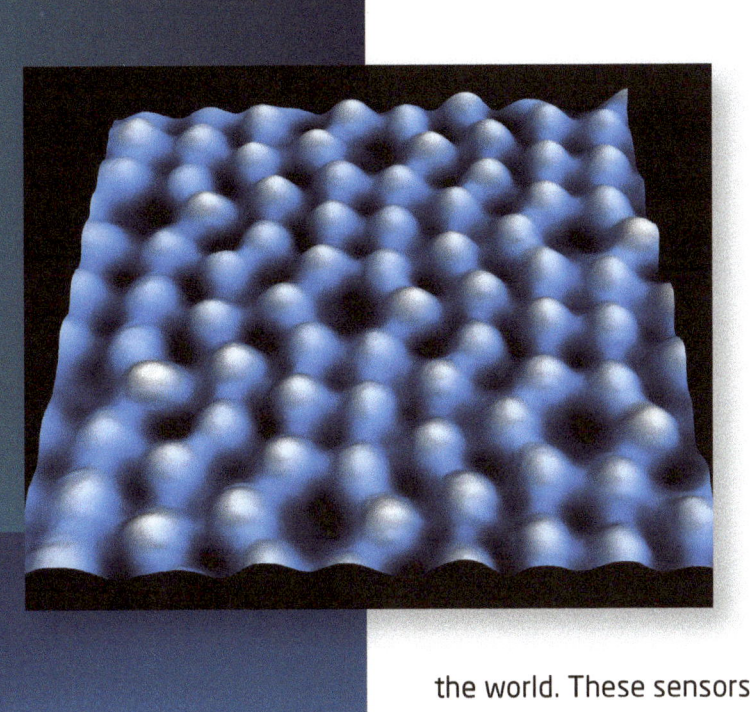

# BETTER DETECTORS

A sensor is any device that gathers useful information from the surroundings. Microscopes, telescopes, and radar are familiar examples of sensor technology. Quantum sensors detect quantum phenomena that occur on the smallest scales—among atoms and subatomic particles. Quantum sensors exploit the fundamental properties of atoms and light to make measurements of the world. These sensors can be incredibly accurate. Quantum sensors that use particles as probes can measure acceleration, magnetic fields, gravity, and the passage of time more precisely than classical devices that are engineered or based on chemical or electrical signals. Quantum sensors can work in locations where classical sensors cannot, such as in the deep ocean or space. Today, quantum sensor technology remains in the early stages of development. But quantum technology promises to revolutionize many areas, including driverless cars, navigation systems, and scientific instruments.

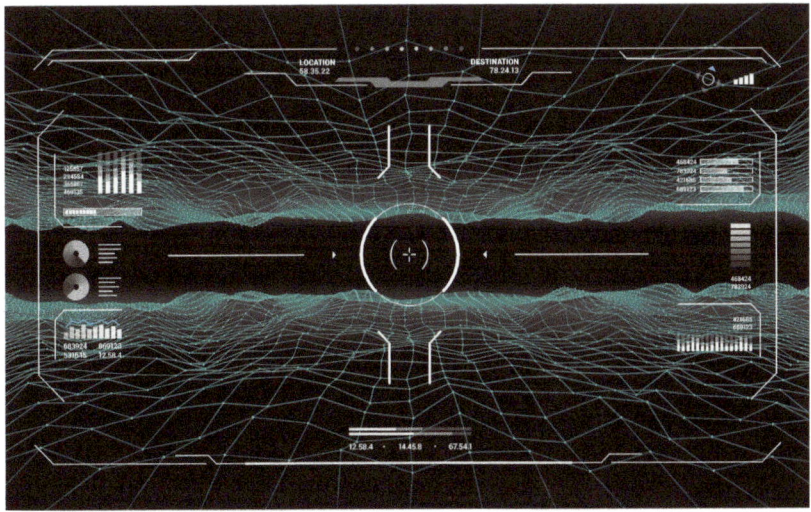

# TUNNELING MICROSCOPES

The electron microscope is not a new piece of technology. It was invented almost one hundred years ago to solve a problem with microscopes that magnified things by focusing light. Microscopes using light cannot focus on objects smaller than about 500 nanometers (500 billionths of a meter). To see things smaller than that, the microscope needs to be one that can image objects using focused beams of electrons—called an electron microscope. The most powerful electron microscope makes use of a quantum phenomenon called quantum tunneling. Known as a scanning tunneling microscope (STM), this device can image objects barely 0.1 nanometers across—it can image individual atoms!

**Quantum tunneling.** The STM detects atoms using a phenomenon called quantum tunneling. The STM brings its probe to within 1 nanometer of the sample and creates a voltage (difference in charge) between the probe and the sample. The voltage creates a tunneling current—an electric current consisting of a flow of electrons between the probe and the sample. That current drops away when the probe is over a gap between the atoms. A computer records the probe's movements and uses them to create an image showing where the atoms are located.

# SCANNING TUNNELING MICROSCOPE

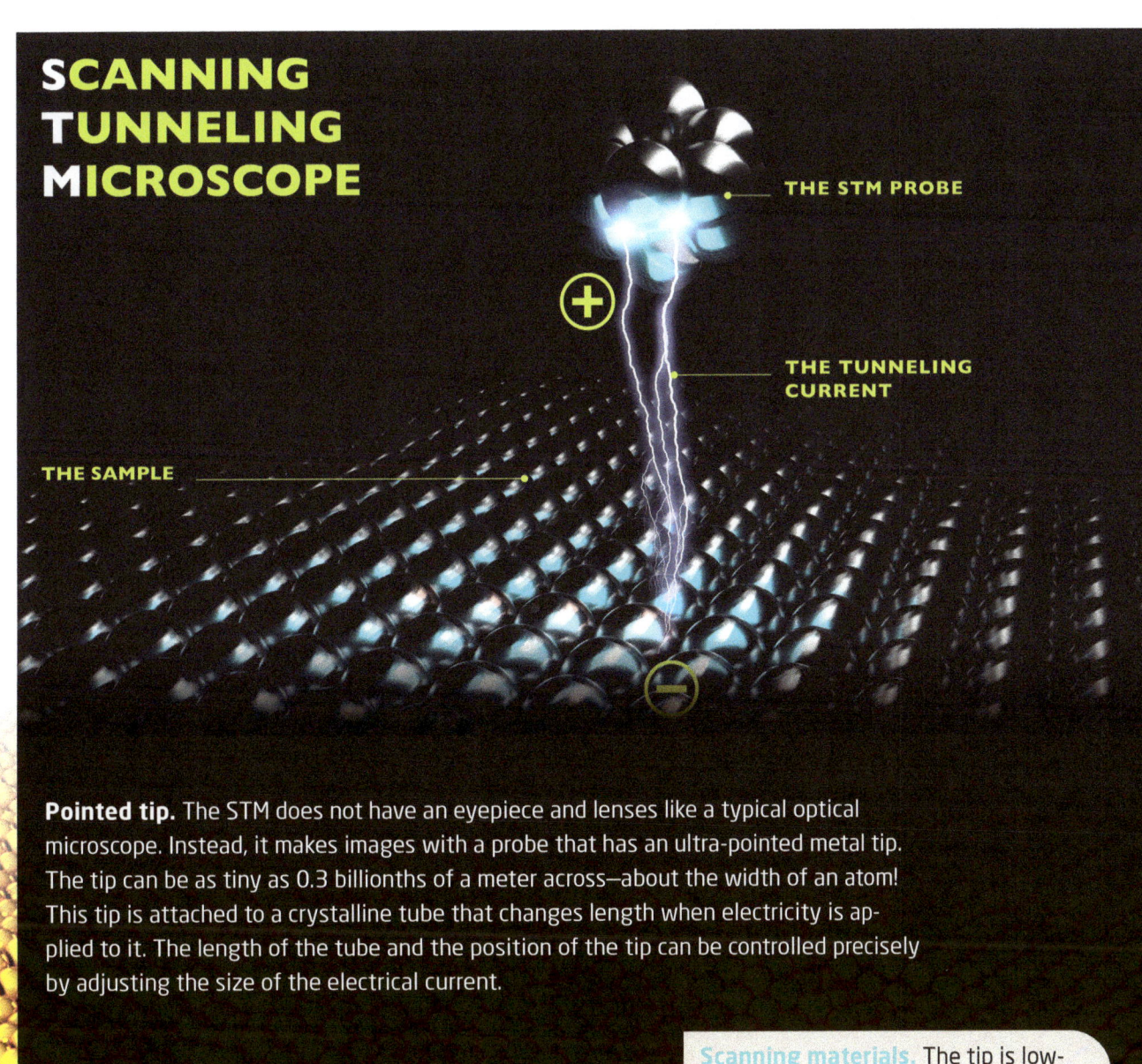

- THE STM PROBE
- THE TUNNELING CURRENT
- THE SAMPLE

**Pointed tip.** The STM does not have an eyepiece and lenses like a typical optical microscope. Instead, it makes images with a probe that has an ultra-pointed metal tip. The tip can be as tiny as 0.3 billionths of a meter across—about the width of an atom! This tip is attached to a crystalline tube that changes length when electricity is applied to it. The length of the tube and the position of the tip can be controlled precisely by adjusting the size of the electrical current.

**Building blocks.** The STM can be used to move atoms as well as image them. The tip is electrified as it nears an atom, and that extra energy allows it to push atoms in the sample one at a time. This technique might be useful in creating advanced electronic components or even quantum dot qubits for use in quantum computers.

**Scanning materials.** The tip is lowered so it is as close as possible to the surface of a material. At the quantum scale, the surface is not smooth but made up of atoms bonded together. The STM moves across the surface and can detect the atoms and the spaces in between. The material and probe are inside a vacuum that is kept very cold. This reduces disruption to the sample and stops activity from outside interfering with the process.

# FINDING THE WAY

Quantum technology is helping improve navigation systems. Any navigation system must be able to determine position and direction of movement and detect objects that may be obstacles. Quantum systems can enhance all aspects of navigation and make it possible to navigate safely in places where today's systems do not work.

**Where am I?** Today, this question is answered using the Global Positioning System (GPS). Devices can use this satellite-based system to pinpoint an exact location just about anywhere on Earth. However, to work properly, the system needs to receive signals from at least three satellites. That is not always possible.

The quantum compass is an alternative to GPS. Quantum compass technology is designed for use on submarines that cannot receive signals from satellites when submerged. A quantum compass precisely tracks motion. A quantum compass will know exactly where it has been and where it is right now—as long as it knows where it started. The system works by reflecting laser beams off super-cold atoms. The laser beams bounce from the atoms in perfect synchronization. When the device moves, the atoms also shift—about the width of one atom. That is enough to change the synchronization of the lasers, which shows up as an interference pattern that indicates the direction of motion.

**Radar and lidar.** These are two technologies able to detect and locate moving or fixed objects. Lidar works on a principle similar to that of radar, but it uses beams of light rather than radio waves. Both can be used by satellites to map the surface of a planet, or they are fitted to self-driving cars to detect hazards on the road. The accuracy and precision of these systems rely on signal quality—which can be improved by quantum tech.

Quantum lidar (also known as quantum radar) is a new advanced sensing technology that uses principles of quantum mechanics to detect objects with great precision. Instead of radio or light waves, these systems use two beams of entangled photons. One beam is directed toward an object. As the beam strikes the target, the entangled photons change their properties. When the signal beam bounces back, it is compared with the other beam. The differences are analyzed and provide information about the target object, such as its distance, shape, and composition, which can be determined with great precision.

# SENSING GRAVITY

A quantum technique called **interferometry** has changed the way astronomers observe the universe. Telescopes can image planets, stars, and galaxies by detecting radiation in the form of visible light, radio waves, ultraviolet, X rays, and even infrared (heat). But the quantum-based Laser Interferometer Gravitational-Wave Observatory (LIGO) detects gravitational waves spreading through space.

**Gravity waves.** Gravity is the force of attraction that acts between all objects because of their mass. An object's mass is its amount of matter. Large objects—such as stars—have a greater force of gravity than smaller objects. When an object moves through space, its gravity squeezes and stretches the space around it. That creates a ripple (wave) in space that travels out in all directions. LIGO detects the gravity waves created by some very heavy objects. The waves give astronomers a new view of space hidden from traditional telescopes.

**Interfering lasers.** The LIGO detectors consist of large interferometers—devices that use lasers to make precise measurements. A LIGO interferometer splits light from a laser into two beams and sends them along separate, perpendicular channels or arms 2.5 miles (4 kilometers) in length. Mirrors at the end of each arm reflect the beams, which come back together at the source. The laser traveling down one path travels exactly half a wavelength farther than the other. This difference means that when the beams meet, they interfere and cancel each other out. There is no laser left.

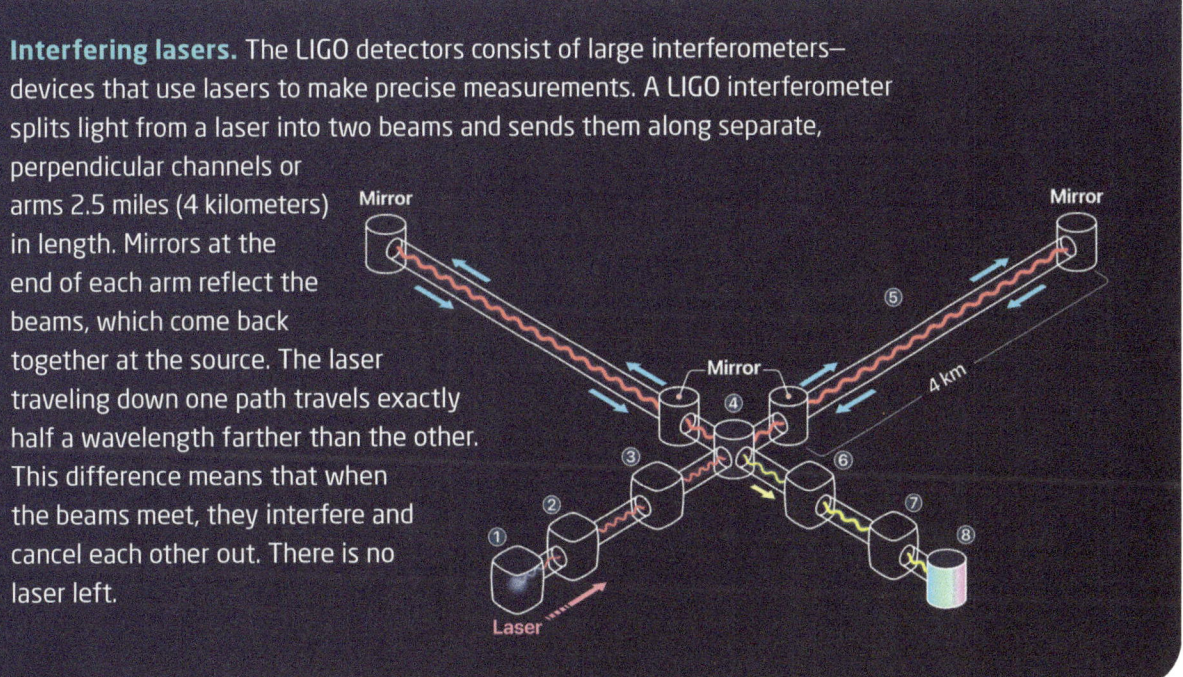

Gravitational waves squeeze and stretch space itself as they move through it. Such a wave passing through a LIGO interferometer changes the length of one arm compared to the other by a tiny amount—less than the width of an atom. The change means the lasers no longer cancel each other and instead create an interference pattern that registers in the LIGO detectors. This interference is a signal of a gravitational wave. LIGO has detected gravitational waves created by violent cosmic events like the collisions of neutron stars, the smallest and densest type of star known. LIGO also detects gravitational waves produced by collisions between black holes, objects whose gravitational force is so strong that nothing can escape.

# 5 QUANTUM COMMUNICATION

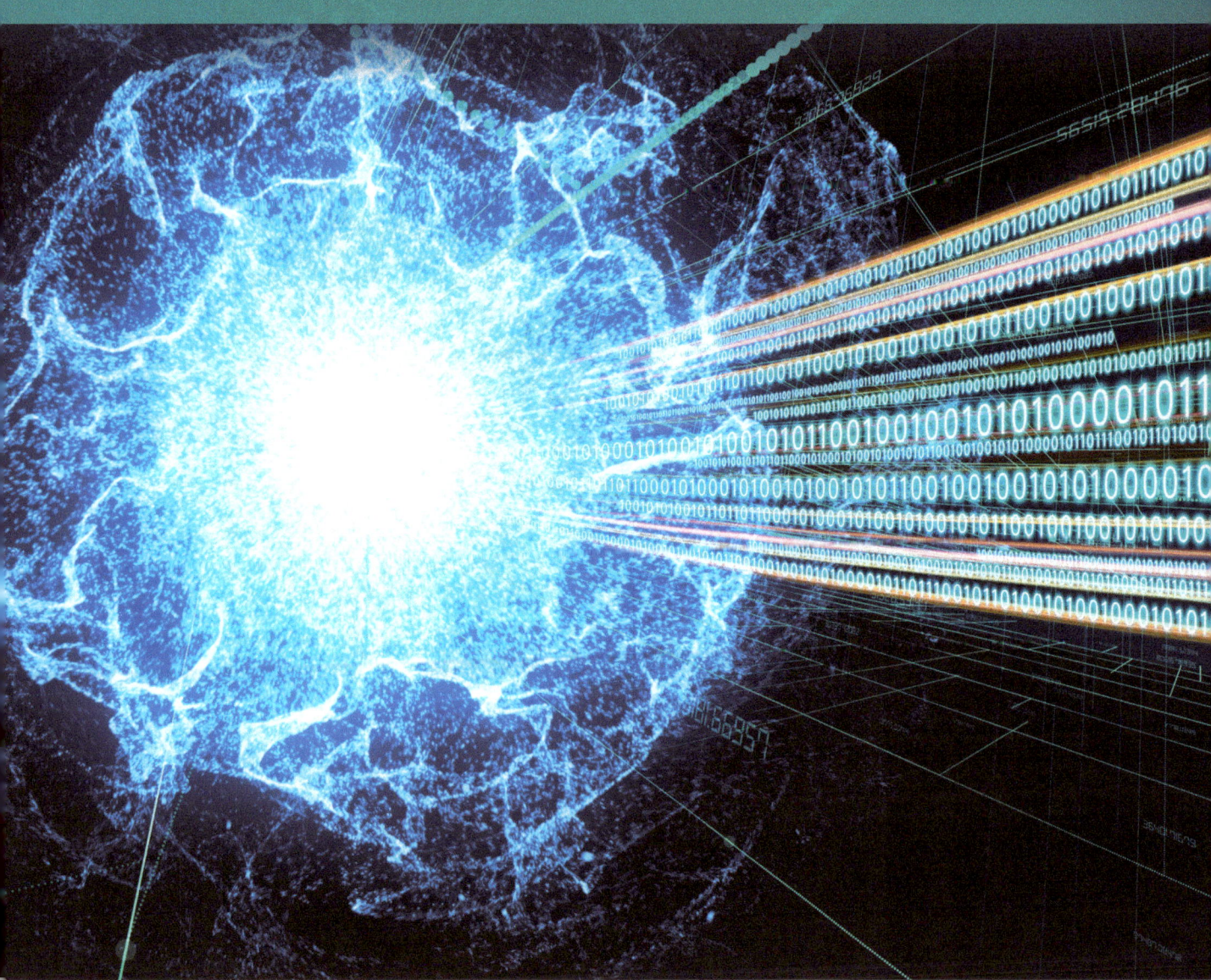

## TALKING IN THE FUTURE

Quantum computing and other tech will change the way we communicate in the future. Some of these changes will not always be welcome. For example, you will soon need a better password to keep your information secure.

Today's computer passwords are not perfect, but a long password will keep your data safe. A typical password with 8 characters can be cracked by a classical computer program in a few minutes, but one that has 12 characters will take several centuries to break. Soon, quantum computers will be capable of cracking those in minutes. In a world where quantum computers are commonplace, you will need to use a 24-character password to have the same level of security as a 12-character password today.

But quantum tech also promises a future with uncrackable encryption that will keep your information safe. Soon, quantum systems could also transform the way we send messages, deliver packages, and even travel—using a futuristic system called quantum **teleportation.**

# QUANTUM ENCRYPTION

Encryption always requires a secret key. Two correspondents sending messages to each other use the same key to code and decode signals. In modern electronic communication, such keys typically exist as long strings of numbers. This key must remain secret even as it is sent in full view of other people. Quantum encryption systems use the phenomenon of entanglement to keep keys safe from the wrong people. The system will also indicate if secret messages are being intercepted.

**Key distribution.** Quantum encryption can use the same mathematical processes used to generate the keys in classical encryption. In a quantum encryption system, the information about the keys is stored and transmitted as qubits rather than as classical bits. In today's classical system, the key's digits are converted into binary—a string of 1's and 0's. That code is transmitted as a flickering pulse of laser light that travels along an optical fiber. This is risky. Smart hackers can read and copy bits in transit without leaving a trace.

**Quantum key.** A quantum key is encoded differently. Secret information about the key is represented by the quantum state of the photons in the laser pulses. The photons exist in a quantum superposition, which means that they represent all combinations of 1 and 0 simultaneously. Quantum encryption keys must be sent through fiber optic connections, so they cannot be used over much of the internet. But experts plan to send encrypted data as classical bits over the internet while the keys to decrypt the information are encoded and transmitted over a separate line as qubits.

**Natural changes.** The quantum key can be sent in plain sight—with no attempt to hide its true meaning. But the information encoded in the qubits will naturally fade away as the delicate quantum superpositions decay. This is a process called quantum decoherence. Currently, the system works best over short distances—which keeps decoherence to a minimum. The longest quantum key communication line today is in China, running more than 1,000 miles (1,600 kilometers) between Shanghai and Beijing.

**Collapsing quantum state.** When a quantum key arrives at the intended destination, the key is decoded. Tests determine how much qubit decoherence has occurred. A great amount of decoherence indicates that a hacker has tried to intercept the key. This feature is due to a strange property of quantum mechanics called the observer paradox—quantum information is always altered whenever it is observed. When the quantum encryption key is read by a hacker, the wave function of the qubits collapses (the entanglements and superpositions disappear). The hacker can never restore the quantum information exactly as it should be.

When the intended receiver gets this damaged message, they know the key is not safe to use for encrypting secrets. They can try again until a key gets through without being intercepted.

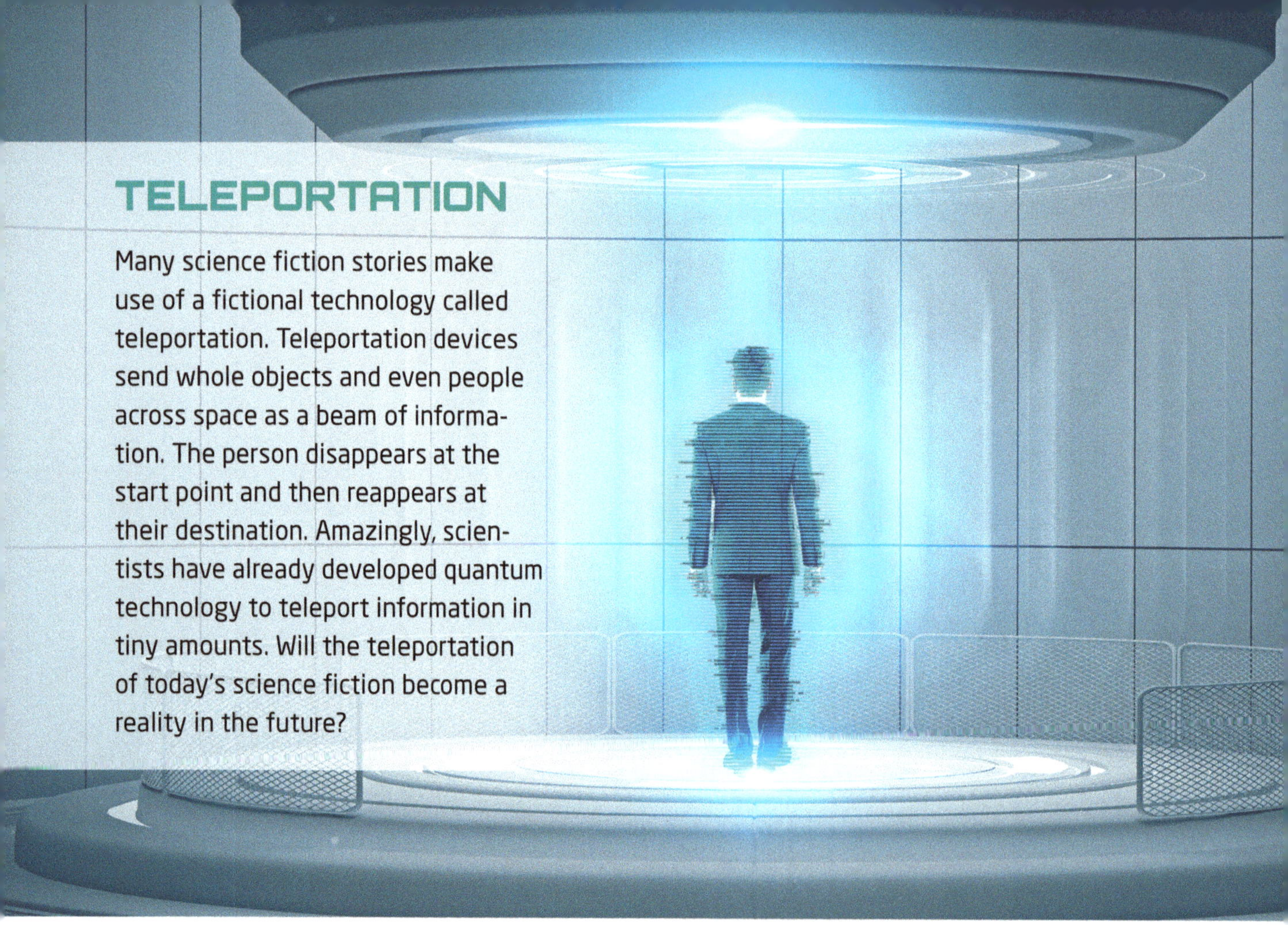

# TELEPORTATION

Many science fiction stories make use of a fictional technology called teleportation. Teleportation devices send whole objects and even people across space as a beam of information. The person disappears at the start point and then reappears at their destination. Amazingly, scientists have already developed quantum technology to teleport information in tiny amounts. Will the teleportation of today's science fiction become a reality in the future?

**Action at a distance.** The teleporters that exist today can only transmit quantum objects—such as an electron or photon—across a space. Quantum teleportation relies on the phenomenon of entanglement. This creates something called action at a distance. If two particles are entangled, an action performed on one of the particles instantly affects the state of the other, even if they are separated by vast distances.

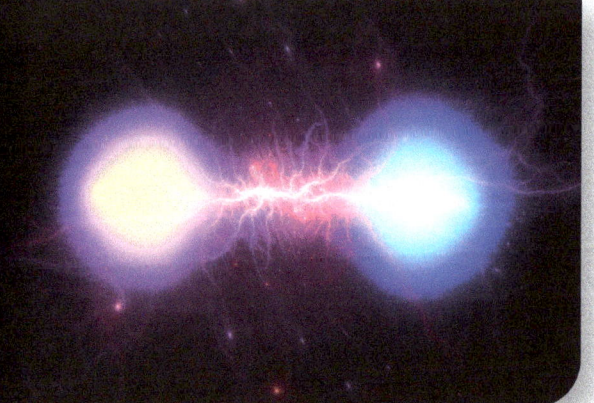

**Quantum teleportation.** Entanglement means that the quantum state of one particle can be transferred to another. In 1992, scientists showed that entanglement could be used to move the state of a quantum particle from one laboratory to another without having to transmit the particle itself. This effect is known as quantum teleportation. Scientists call it teleportation because the second particle is identical to the original one, and so it is as if the particle itself has traveled from one place to another.

**Faster than light.** The amazing thing about entanglement and quantum teleportation is that when one particle changes, the other changes at the same time. The information travels between the two in an instant no matter how far away they are. In our everyday experience, nothing can travel faster than light, even information. But quantum teleportation systems still require some information sent as classical bits. These have to be sent by radio or laser pulses that travel at or below the speed of light. So as the system works now, it is not possible to teleport information or objects faster than the speed of light.

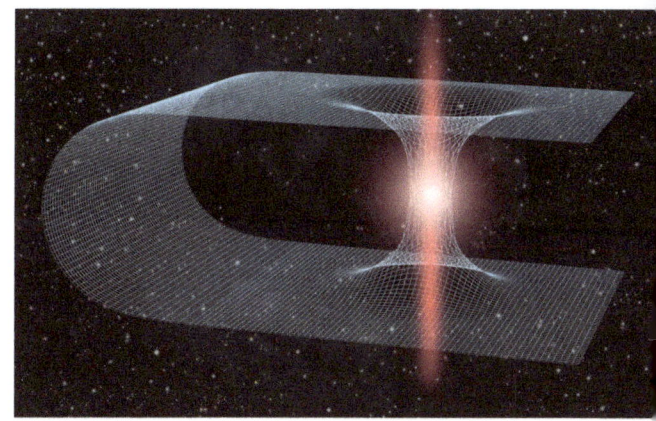

**Teleportation.** In theory, it may be possible to send an object or even a person somewhere through teleportation. But it would not be easy. A person is made up of trillions of particles—each one with a particular quantum state. To teleport a person, a transporter machine must capture and teleport every entangled particle. The teleportation part certainly works, but capturing the quantum state of each particle is more complicated.

One futuristic proposal is to make the object to be teleported a quantum condensate—an extremely cold substance where the atoms merge into a liquid-like quantum substance. In this exotic form of matter, all the atoms act as a single quantum object. In theory, that quantum information could be collected and transmitted to another teleporter that rebuilds the object from different particles. The theory sounds great, but such technology may never happen. A lot could go wrong. For now, teleportation remains science fiction. Quantum tech will not change the way we travel any time soon. But, who knows what kind of future awaits as quantum tech becomes reality?

# ENGAGE YOUR READER

Nonfiction writing often includes subject-specific vocabulary terms. Knowing the words related to the topic helps us understand the text itself.

When good readers come upon words they don't know well, they pause and try to figure them out. One tool they use is the glossary, like the one on page 4. Not every word can be defined in a glossary, though!

Authors know this, so they leave clues about words in the text. Next time you encounter a challenging word, stop and look for information about its meaning in the surrounding sentences. Sometimes authors define the term right there in the text! Other times, they'll compare the term to something you may already know. Authors even use punctuation like commas or dashes to clue you in to a word's meaning.

## INSTRUCTIONS

1. Consider the list of challenge words and identify where each is used in the text. You can use the Index on page 48 to help you locate each term.

2. Explain how the author described each word. Ask yourself "what is happening in the text?" or "how is this word being used?" as you search for clues about their meanings.

3. Create your own definitions of the words. Don't just copy the dictionary definitions. Instead think about how you would tell a friend what each term means.

4. Add a visual representation for each word. Think about what you could draw that will help you remember what the words mean.

Visit www.worldbook.com/resources to download your own graphic organizer as well as other free resources!

## CHALLENGE WORDS

- Subatomic
- Silicon
- Superconductor
- Processor
- Transistor
- Nanometer
- Nucleus
- Microchip

# EXAMPLE

| Challenge Word | Page(s) | Author's Description | Personal Definition | Visual Representation |
|---|---|---|---|---|
| Subatomic | 8-9, 11, 15, 28, 30, 33 | - particles called protons and neutrons<br>- electrons<br>- a photon that makes up light | A piece of matter that is smaller than an atom. | |
| Silicon | | | | |

# INDEX

## A
absolute zero, 14, 28
algorithm, 17, 18, 19, 22
artificial intelligence (AI), 7, 12, 19, 22
atoms, 5, 7, 8, 9, 11, 15, 27, 28, 29, 30, 33, 34, 35, 36, 39, 45

## B
bits, 10, 11, 12, 13, 15, 42, 43, 45
byte, 13

## C
China, 30, 43
Chinese Academy of Science, 24
circuit, 8, 11
Circular Electron Positron Collider (CEPC), 30
classical computer, 7, 8, 9, 10, 11, 12, 13, 17, 18, 19, 21, 23, 24, 25, 33, 41, 42, 43, 45
communication, 5, 20, 42, 43
consciousness, 23

## D
data, 12, 13, 14, 15, 19, 20, 22, 23, 25, 41, 43
decoherence, 43
driverless cars, 33

## E
electron microscope, 34
electrons, 8, 9, 11, 15, 34, 35, 44
encryption, 20, 21, 41, 42, 43

## G
gigabytes, 13
Google, 19, 24
gravitational waves, 38, 39

## H
hacker, 43
hard problems, 18

## I
IBM, 14, 24
Intel, 24, 25
interferometry, 38
internet, 12, 19, 20, 43

## K
kilobytes, 13

## L
Large Hadron Collider (LHC), 30
laser beams, 25, 36
Laser Interferometer Gravitational-Wave Observatory (LIGO), 38
lidar, 37

## M
machine learning, 22, 23
mathematics, 7, 9, 10, 18, 23, 29
megabytes, 13
memory, 13, 25, 29
microchip, 5, 10, 13, 15
Microsoft, 24

## N
nanometers, 5, 34, 35
nucleus, 8

## O
observer paradox, 43

## P
particle accelerator, 30
password, 41
photonics, 15
photons, 25, 28, 37, 43
processing power, 13, 21, 23
processor, 5, 10, 11, 12, 13, 14, 15, 21, 22, 23, 24, 25
program, computer, 10, 11, 17, 19, 20, 22, 23, 41

## Q
quantum algorithms, 19
quantum annealing, 19
quantum compass, 36
quantum entanglement, 11, 23, 28, 42, 44, 45
quantum mechanics, 5, 8, 9, 10, 17, 23, 27, 28, 29, 30, 31, 33, 37, 43
quantum phenomenon, 11, 29, 34
quantum practicality, 25
quantum sensor, 33
quantum simulator, 28
quantum supremacy, 24, 25
quantum tunneling, 19, 23, 34, 35
qubit, 11, 13, 14, 15, 17, 21, 23, 24, 25, 28, 35, 42, 43

## R
radar, 33, 37
random access memory, 25
resistance, 28

## S
scanning tunneling microscope (STM), 34-35
security, 20, 21, 41
silicon, 7, 8, 15, 25
smartphones, 12, 14
standard model, 31
subatomic particles, 8, 9, 11, 15, 28, 30, 33
superconductor, 14, 15, 24, 28, 30
superfluid, 29
superposition, 11, 17, 23, 43

## T
technological singularity, 23
technology, 5, 7, 12, 17, 21, 24, 27, 33, 34, 36, 37, 44, 45
teleportation, 41, 44, 45
temperature, 14, 28, 29
time crystal, 29
transistors, 8, 11, 15
Turing, Alan, 18

## U
uncertainty principle, 9

## V
voltage, 15, 35

www.ingramcontent.com/pod-product-compliance
Lightning Source LLC
Chambersburg PA
CBHW041138170426
43198CB00023B/2985